D1603252

Heroes for Young Readers

Written by Renee Taft Meloche
Illustrated by Bryan Pollard

Adoniram Judson	Gladys Aylward
Amy Carmichael	Hudson Taylor
Betty Greene	Ida Scudder
Brother Andrew	Jim Elliot
Cameron Townsend	Jonathan Goforth
Corrie ten Boom	Loren Cunningham
C. S. Lewis	Lottie Moon
David Livingstone	Mary Slessor
Eric Liddell	Nate Saint
George Müller	William Carey

Heroes of History for Young Readers

Written by Renee Taft Meloche
Illustrated by Bryan Pollard

Daniel Boone
Clara Barton
George Washington
George Washington Carver
Meriwether Lewis

...and more coming soon

*Heroes for Young Readers Activity Guides and audio CDs
are now available! See the back of this book for more information.*

For a free catalog of books and materials contact
YWAM Publishing, P.O. Box 55787, Seattle, WA 98155
1-800-922-2143 www.ywampublishing.com

HEROES FOR YOUNG READERS

IDA SCUDDER

Healing in India

Written by Renee Taft Meloche
Illustrated by Bryan Pollard

YWAM PUBLISHING

P.O. BOX 55787   SEATTLE, WA 98155

Ida Scudder: Healing in India   Text © 2009 by Renee Taft Meloche   Illustrations © 2009 by Bryan Pollard
Published by YWAM Publishing, P.O. Box 55787, Seattle, WA 98155   ISBN 978-1-57658-472-9   Printed in China.   All rights reserved.

A young girl, Ida Scudder, loved
    her new Nebraska home
with wide and open countryside
    where she was free to roam.

The year was eighteen seventy-eight
    and Ida longed to stay.
She'd lived for years in India,
    a country far away.

Her mother and her father had
    been missionaries there.
Her father, though, got sick and needed
    rest and clean fresh air.

In India, the weather could
    get hot with humid heat.
And many on the streets wore rags
    and begged for food to eat.

Her father, as a doctor, helped
    those needing to be fed.
And Ida helped him too by handing
    out some chunks of bread.

But now she rode her horse around
    Nebraska's open space,
and thought, *I like America*
    more than I like that place.
The air is fresh, the smells are sweet.
    This is the life for me,
away from all that suffering
    and endless poverty.

So when her parents both returned
    to India to live,
young Ida chose to stay behind
    with nearby relatives.

She grew and went to college, then
    her father sent her news:
"Please come. Your mother's very ill
    and needs some help from you."

So Ida sailed to India
    where there was much to do.
She nursed her mother and helped run
    a school for young boys too.

But secretly she longed to leave—
    America was home.
She hoped to marry and enjoy
    the comforts she had known.

One evening, at her door, a rich
     young Indian man appeared.
As he stood shaking, Ida thought,
     What is he doing here?

"The baby that my wife is having
     will not come!" he cried.
"I've heard that you can help her, so
     please hurry or she'll die."

Yet Ida paused and shook her head.
     "I cannot help," she said.
"My father is a doctor, though,
     and he can help instead."

"But my religion won't permit
     a man to touch my wife.
So all is lost then," he replied.
     "No one can save her life."

He left and Ida felt so bad.
    Then after a short time,
she heard footsteps again and thought,
    Perhaps he's changed his mind.

But, no, another man stood there.
    He said, "I am in need.
The baby that my wife is having
    won't come naturally.
I hear there is a doctor." Ida
    nodded, turned, and ran.
She brought her father, but the man
    said, "You don't understand."

"No man can touch my wife, but I
    have heard—is it not true?—
that you, too, are a doctor and
    will know just what to do?"

"I'm not a doctor," Ida said.
    The hope drained from his face.
"Then she will die," he said and frowned,
    then bowed and left the place.

At that same place, another man
    appeared that very night.
"My wife's in labor," he explained,
    "and something is not right."

When Ida offered to go get
    her father's help for him,
he shook his head, then turned around
    and headed home again.

As Ida tossed in bed that night,
    she thought of all three wives:
*There are no female doctors here
    to help save women's lives.*

When in the morning tom-toms beat,
    her fears were realized:
three women had tried giving birth
    and each of them had died.

To her the loss seemed senseless, and
    the husbands were in grief.
She knew they were just honoring
    their customs and beliefs.

So moved was Ida that she thought
    about a new career.
She prayed, "Lord, help me spend my life
    assisting women here."

This meant she had to let go of
    the easy life she'd planned,
to help those who so needed her,
    the ones there in that land.

So Ida—once her mother was
     completely well again—
returned home to America
     to study medicine.

And after many years of study,
     she got her degree.
Then Doctor Ida Scudder sailed
     for weeks across the seas
to India, where she began
     a women's clinic there
in eighteen ninety-nine to help
     give women better care.

A hospital was planned and built
    within the next two years.
A famine had hit India,
    a famine so severe
that people walked one hundred miles,
    starving, sickly thin,
to get to Ida's hospital
    in hopes she'd take them in.

She nursed the sick and fed the poor,
    and when one year had passed,
the rains came down and crops began
    to grow again at last.

One morning at the hospital,
	she pushed open a door
to visit one sick baby girl
	and check on her once more.

She saw the baby's grandmother—
	and her mother too—
just stand there and not help the baby,
	who was turning blue!

So Ida rushed in quickly and
	massaged the baby's chest
until her breathing was okay
	again and she could rest.

Then Ida asked them why they had
	not helped in any way.
"The baby," said the grandmother,
	"was born on the wrong day—
a day that is not lucky, so
	it's our god's will she dies."
"Please take her," said the mother.
	Ida stared at them, surprised.

So Ida took the girl into
    her care, and as she grew
she turned into a happy child.
    Then Ida heard the news
that three more babies needed homes.
    She could not turn away,
and took these babies in as well
    and cared for them each day.

One morning at the hospital
    a boy came in, in pain.
He had a large growth on his leg,
    and Ida worked in vain.

She sadly told his mother, "You
    have brought him here too late.
You knew he was in pain for days—
    whatever made you wait?"

"I could not come," she answered her,
    "for everyone I knew
told me it simply was an image
    of a god, which grew.
They said if I removed the growth,
    the god would be quite mad."
The words the woman spoke to her
    made Ida very sad.

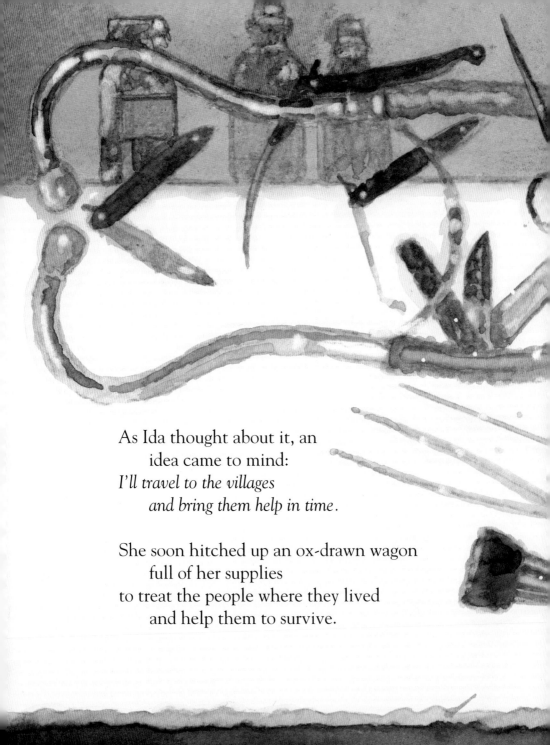

As Ida thought about it, an
    idea came to mind:
I'll travel to the villages
    and bring them help in time.

She soon hitched up an ox-drawn wagon
    full of her supplies
to treat the people where they lived
    and help them to survive.

She met an old man by the road
    who said, "It's hard to hear.
I paid a man to take out flies
    he said buzzed in my ear.
I have no money left to get
    more flies removed from me."
So Ida peered into his ear
    for problems she could see.

And through her magnifying glass
    she saw in his eardrum
a pebble, which she took with tweezers.
    She was quickly done.

The man was so relieved there was
    no buzzing anymore.
Although no flies had been removed,
    his hearing was restored.

These roadside stops soon drew large crowds
     of people, sick and lame,
who'd wait for her beside the road
     to help them when she came.

Before she treated anyone,
     she'd start out with a prayer
and talk about her Christian faith
     out in the open air.

At first she rode by wagon to
     the roadside crowds in need,
but then received a gift—a car—
     to travel more in ease.

Since cars were just invented, though,
     and rarely ever seen,
when Ida drove up to a village,
     people ran and screamed.

However, many soon returned—
     a steady, constant stream
of people who got used to Ida's
     noisy, strange machine.

At one small village Ida noticed
    under people's skin
worms that wriggled all about—
    long and white and thin.

She showed the people water and
    said, "Take a look and see
the tiny white worms moving in
    the water constantly.
And when you drink it, they can get
    inside your bodies too,
where they will grow and grow and grow.
    So here's what you must do:
just pour your water through a cloth—
    what you will drink that day—
and it will catch the worms and you
    can safely drink that way."

Since Ida needed help in caring
    for those who were ill,
she built a women's nursing school
    to teach some basic skills.

The women then could go and work
    throughout their native land,
assisting on the roadsides and
    in hospitals as planned.

And once she'd taught them nursing skills,
    she thought, *There's such a need
for women doctors to be trained.*
    Determined to succeed,
she started up a school for fourteen
    Indian women who
then took a medical exam
    when their first year was through.

Though men from schools around the country
    often failed the test,
all fourteen of the women passed—
    the brightest and the best.

Then four years later they achieved
    a wonderful breakthrough,
for now they were new doctors!
    Ida's vision had come true.

At ninety years of age, in nineteen
    sixty, Ida died.
Her hospital and schools are still
    well known today worldwide
for their great care and excellence.
    And patients, while they stay,
can hear some Bible stories and
    with others also pray.

Young Ida once had plans of how
    she thought she'd like to live,
but then gave up a life of ease
    so she could freely give.

We too can find our special gifts.
    And when we see a need,
we too can make a difference as
    we follow our God's lead.

Christian Heroes: Then & Now

by Janet and Geoff Benge

Adoniram Judson: Bound for Burma
Amy Carmichael: Rescuer of Precious Gems
Betty Greene: Wings to Serve
Brother Andrew: God's Secret Agent
Cameron Townsend: Good News in Every Language
Clarence Jones: Mr. Radio
Corrie ten Boom: Keeper of the Angels' Den
Count Zinzendorf: Firstfruit
C. S. Lewis: Master Storyteller
C. T. Studd: No Retreat
David Bussau: Facing the World Head-on
David Livingstone: Africa's Trailblazer
Eric Liddell: Something Greater Than Gold
Florence Young: Mission Accomplished
George Müller: The Guardian of Bristol's Orphans
Gladys Aylward: The Adventure of a Lifetime
Hudson Taylor: Deep in the Heart of China
Ida Scudder: Healing Bodies, Touching Hearts
Jacob DeShazer: Forgive Your Enemies
Jim Elliot: One Great Purpose
John Wesley: The World His Parish
John Williams: Messenger of Peace
Jonathan Goforth: An Open Door in China
Lillian Trasher: The Greatest Wonder in Egypt
Loren Cunningham: Into All the World
Lottie Moon: Giving Her All for China
Mary Slessor: Forward into Calabar
Nate Saint: On a Wing and a Prayer
Rachel Saint: A Star in the Jungle
Rowland Bingham: Into Africa's Interior
Sundar Singh: Footprints Over the Mountains
Wilfred Grenfell: Fisher of Men
William Booth: Soup, Soap, and Salvation
William Carey: Obliged to Go

Heroes for Young Readers and Heroes of History for Young Readers are based on the Christian Heroes: Then & Now and Heroes of History biographies by Janet and Geoff Benge. Don't miss out on these exciting, true adventures for ages ten and up!

Continued on the next page...

Heroes of History

by Janet and Geoff Benge

Abraham Lincoln: A New Birth of Freedom
Alan Shepard: Higher and Faster
Benjamin Franklin: Live Wire
Christopher Columbus: Across the Ocean Sea
Clara Barton: Courage under Fire
Daniel Boone: Frontiersman
Douglas MacArthur: What Greater Honor
George Washington Carver: From Slave to Scientist
George Washington: True Patriot
Harriet Tubman: Freedombound
John Adams: Independence Forever
John Smith: A Foothold in the New World
Laura Ingalls Wilder: A Storybook Life
Meriwether Lewis: Off the Edge of the Map
Orville Wright: The Flyer
Theodore Roosevelt: An American Original
Thomas Edison: Inspiration and Hard Work
William Penn: Liberty and Justice for All

...and more coming soon. Unit Study Curriculum Guides are also available.

Heroes for Young Readers Activity Guides
Educational and Character-Building Lessons for Children

by Renee Taft Meloche

Heroes for Young Readers Activity Guide for Books 1–4
Gladys Aylward, Eric Liddell, Nate Saint, George Müller

Heroes for Young Readers Activity Guide for Books 5–8
Amy Carmichael, Corrie ten Boom, Mary Slessor, William Carey

Heroes for Young Readers Activity Guide for Books 9–12
Betty Greene, David Livingstone, Adoniram Judson, Hudson Taylor

Heroes for Young Readers Activity Guide for Books 13–16
Jim Elliot, Cameron Townsend, Jonathan Goforth, Lottie Moon
Heroes of History for Young Readers Activity Guide for Books 1–4
George Washington Carver, Meriwether Lewis, George Washington, Clara Barton

...and more coming soon.

Designed to accompany the vibrant Heroes for Young Readers books, these fun-filled Activity Guides lead young children through a variety of character-building and educational activities. Pick and choose from the activities or follow the included thirteen-week syllabus. An audio CD with book readings, songs, and fun activity tracks is available for each Activity Guide.

For a free catalog of books and materials contact
YWAM Publishing, P.O. Box 55787, Seattle, WA 98155
1-800-922-2143 www.ywampublishing.com